OSCAR DE LA HOYA

A Real-Life Reader Biography

Valerie Menard

Mitchell Lane Publishers, Inc.
P.O. Box 200 • Childs, Maryland 21916

Second Printing

Real-Life Reader Biographies

Selena	Robert Rodriguez	Mariah Carey	Rafael Palmeiro
Tommy Nuñez	Trent Dimas	Cristina Saralegui	Andres Galarraga
Oscar De La Hoya	Gloria Estefan	Jimmy Smits	Mary Joe Fernandez
Cesar Chavez	Celine Dion	Vanessa Williams	Sinbad
Sammy Sosa	Brandy	Paula Abdul	Chuck Norris
Mia Hamm	Shania Twain	Garth Brooks	Jeff Gordon

Library of Congress Cataloging-in-Publication Data
Menard, Valerie.
    Oscar De la Hoya / Valerie Menard.
        p. cm.—(A real-life reader biography)
    Includes index.
    Summary: Traces the life of the young Mexican-American boxer who won a gold medal at the 1992 Olympic Games at the age of nineteen and went on to win numerous professional boxing titles.
        ISBN 1-883845-58-0 (lib. bound)
    1. De la Hoya, Oscar, 1973- —Juvenile literature. 2. Boxers (Sports)—United States—Biography—Juvenile literature. [1. De la Hoya, Oscar, 1973- . 2. Boxers (Sports) 3. Mexican Americans—Biography.] I. Title. II. Series.
GV1132.D37M45 1998
796.83'092—dc21   97-43509
[B]   CIP
                                                                                                                 AC

ABOUT THE AUTHOR: Valerie Menard has been an editor for *Hispanic* magazine since the magazine moved to Austin, Texas, in July 1994. Before joining the magazine, she was a managing editor of a bilingual weekly, *La Prensa*. She is a contributing writer to the Mitchell Lane series **Famous People of Hispanic Heritage**. Valerie writes from a Latino perspective and as an advocate for Latino causes.

PHOTO CREDITS: cover: Reuters/Marsh Starks/Archive Photos; p. 4 sketch by Barbara Tidman; pp. 9 and 14 Globe Photos/Lisa Rose; p. 15 Globe Photos/Rose Hartman; p. 17 Reuters/Neal Lauron/Archive Photos; p. 18 AP Photo/Jeff Scheid; pp. 21 and 22 AP Photo/Lennox McLendon

ACKNOWLEDGMENTS: The following story has been thoroughly researched and checked for accuracy. To the best of our knowledge, it represents a true story. Though we attempt to contact each person in our Real-Life Reader Biographies, for various reasons, we were unable to authorize every story.

Table of Contents

Chapter 1
Golden Boy

Oscar De La Hoya, or the Golden Boy, as he's known by his fans, should feel proud. By the time he was 24 years old, he had done a lot. He had won a gold medal in boxing at the 1992 Summer Olympics. In 1996 he became the World Boxing Council (WBC) champion of the world in the super lightweight division. He did this by beating his idol, Julio Cesar Chavez, the great Mexican fighter. The victory took his boxing record to

Oscar is known by his fans as the Golden Boy.

23–0: 23 wins with no losses. Oscar won three more fights since then and still hasn't stopped dreaming. He's still the same wide-eyed boy who was in Barcelona, Spain, at the 1992 Summer Olympics. "I fight first for my mother, then my family, then myself, then for all the people who support me—the Mexican people, all Hispanic people," says Oscar. "I fight for the whole world."

Oscar grew up in East Los Angeles.

Oscar's parents are Joel and Cecilia De La Hoya. Growing up in East Los Angeles, Oscar was the middle child. He was born in 1973; his brother, Joel Jr., was born in 1971; and his sister, Cecilia, was born in 1982.

Oscar's father first took him to the gym and encouraged him to take up boxing when he was just six years old. Oscar's grandfather,

Vicente, had been a boxer, and Joel had also boxed professionally for a short time. It wasn't long before Oscar had his first boxing match. Because his family could not afford new equipment, everything Oscar wore into the ring was borrowed. The gloves were too large, and his shoes, borrowed from his uncle, were five sizes too big. "I looked like a clown, with the fronts [of my shoes] all curling up," he remembers. "But I stopped a kid in the first round. That's when my father said, 'He's gonna be a big champion!'"

His father and his grandfather had both been boxers.

Chapter 2
A Mother's Love

Oscar wanted to win a gold medal in the Olympics for his mother.

The Barcelona Games were not the best Olympics for the United States Boxing Team. Many of the boxers who were supposed to win, lost. Reporters began to focus more and more on young Oscar. It looked as if he would be the only one on the team who would win a medal. But Oscar was on a greater, more personal mission. He was going to win the gold medal for his mother, Cecilia, who had died of breast cancer two years before the Olympics, on October 28, 1990.

Cecilia had always supported her son's ambition. She hid her illness from Oscar so that he wouldn't worry. He discovered that his mother was dying only two days before she passed away. She was only 39. "[My parents] didn't tell me before how sick she was because they didn't want it to affect my boxing," he remembers. "But she'd gotten so sick I began to worry." It was then that he made a vow to his mother to win the gold medal.

Oscar won a gold medal in the 1992 Olympics in Barcelona, Spain.

One day, Oscar decided to quit boxing. "I was tired of it. I wanted to be a regular, normal kid," he says.

"Her dream was for me to go to the Olympic Games," Oscar says. "That's what motivated me. It was easier after that. I was untouchable. I was invincible."

Oscar almost didn't make it to the Olympics. When he was about ten, he skipped gym one day and joined the other kids in the neighborhood. They were riding their skateboards. When his father found out, he went after Oscar and ordered him back into the gym. A year later, Oscar decided to quit boxing. "I was tired of it. I wanted to be with friends, just hang out, be like a regular, normal kid," he says. But after only six months, he returned to the gym. "I missed it," he says.

In school, Oscar did well in drafting and art classes. In 1992, he graduated from Garfield High School in East Los Angeles.

More and more, De La Hoya seemed to identify with being a boxer. He was very good at it and it made his parents proud. As an amateur fighter, De La Hoya built a fight record of 225 wins and five losses. He was only 17 when his mother died, but she had already told him how important it was for him to compete in the Olympics, and Oscar had worked too hard to give up.

Oscar was only 17 when his mother died.

Chapter 3
The Olympic Games

Many boxers started their careers by winning in the Olympics.

Many professional boxers started their careers by winning gold medals at the Olympic Games. De La Hoya hoped to add his name to the list that includes Sugar Ray Leonard, Leon Spinks, and Muhammad Ali.

De La Hoya beat Adilson Silva of Brazil, Moses Odion of Nigeria, Dimitrov Tontchev of Bulgaria, and Hong Sun Sik of South Korea before reaching the gold medal round, where he faced a long-time enemy,

German fighter Marco Rudolph. Rudolph had beaten De La Hoya the year before in Australia at the World Amateur Boxing Championships. This time, however, De La Hoya's luck would change. He beat Rudolph and won the only gold medal for the U.S. Boxing Team at that Olympics.

When he won, Oscar ran around the ring holding up two flags, one from Mexico, the other from the United States. De La Hoya says, "I went up [to the Olympics] with the Mexican flag and the American flag. If I'd had enough arms I would have gone up with all the flags of the world." When he walked up to the medal stand, received his gold medal, and listened to "The Star Spangled Banner" begin to play, he thought of his mother and it nearly made

Oscar won the only gold medal for the U.S. Boxing Team in Barcelona.

him cry. "I was afraid I might start to cry," he admits, "but then I figured my mom would say, 'Don't cry, be happy—you won the gold medal.'"

Oscar received a contract from HBO to televise his fights.

After the Olympics, Oscar had very different plans. He wanted to return to school and study architecture. But his father—and several boxing promoters—had other plans. Within the year, Oscar had already been offered a $21 million contract by Home Box Office (HBO) to show his fights on cable television. Still only 19 years old, De La Hoya had a lot to consider. "I started to realize that I had to think about my future," he says. "I had to think about if [my mother] were here, how she would want my life to progress. I had to think about all the people who helped me, so I could pay them back." So, instead of college, De La Hoya kept boxing.

Oscar helped celebrate HBO's 200th fight.

Chapter 4
Professional Boxer

Oscar's first professional fight was in 1992.

Oscar fought his first professional fight as a lightweight on November 23, 1992. It was at that fight that he was given his nickname, the Golden Boy, by boxing announcer Jimmy Lennon Jr. He fought against Lamar Williams. Oscar won that fight in one minute and 42 seconds by a knockout punch. That victory earned him $150,000. Years later, De La Hoya would earn $8.5 million in his victory against Chavez.

Going from poverty to sudden fame and fortune wasn't easy. Remembering how much he liked skateboards, the first thing Oscar bought was several brand-new ones. He also helped his family. He bought them a four-bedroom house in Montebello, California. But Oscar spent a lot of his first $1 million contract.

Oscar (right) lands a jab on Julio Cesar Chavez at Caesars Palace in Las Vegas, June 7, 1996. De La Hoya beat Chavez after the fight was stopped in the fourth round.

Referee Mitch Halpern holds Oscar's arm up after he won a fight against Darryl Tyson on February 9, 1996, in Las Vegas. Oscar won the bout in the second round with a knockout to take the junior welterweight title.

Even Oscar and his father fought because of the money. He and his father have since become close again. Joel Sr. will always be Oscar's first hero, but today Oscar also takes advice from Mike Hernandez. Hernandez is a successful businessman who helps young Latinos, mostly athletes. He taught Oscar about business and told him to be careful with his money.

Hernandez told Oscar that there was no reason he couldn't manage his own career, and that's what Oscar did. "I'm not gonna be another statistic in boxing," asserts Oscar. "They're not going to say, 'He's just another fighter like any of the others: He made money, he lost it, and didn't make [anything] of himself.'"

Oscar had to learn how to manage all the money he made. It was not easy to go from being poor to having lots of money.

Chapter 5
Home Boy

Oscar hasn't forgotten his roots. He keeps a food stamp in his wallet to make sure he doesn't forget. He often returns to East Los Angeles to speak to young people about the importance of education and self-esteem. "I go back to schools to speak to kids about their futures. Just because they are Hispanic, they shouldn't feel left out or below someone else—we should all feel equal. I grew up without having anything in life: I

Oscar still carries a food stamp in his wallet so that he'll remember where he came from.

had to struggle, so I can relate to them," says Oscar. He has also given back to his old neighborhood. He has scholarships in his name, and he fixed up an old gym in East Los Angeles. It is now called the

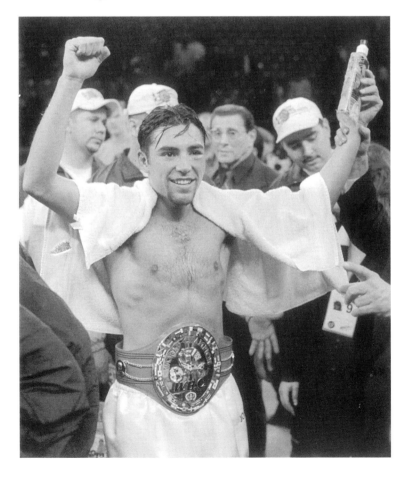

Oscar successfully defended his super lightweight title against Miguel Angel Gonzalez on January 18, 1997, in Las Vegas.

"I want to be considered as one of the great legends who fought the best and beat the best," said Oscar in a news conference in Jan. 1997.

Oscar De La Hoya Boxing Youth Center.

De La Hoya has won five titles. Before beating Chavez and winning the WBC super lightweight title, he beat Ruelas for the International Boxing Federation (IBF) lightweight crown. Before that he beat Jorge Paez for the World Boxing Organization (WBO) junior lightweight title while holding the WBO lightweight title. With each bout, De La Hoya gets closer to his ultimate goal of

being the first Hispanic boxer to win titles across six weight divisions. He earned his fifth crown against Pernell Whitaker, whom he defeated in 1997; Whitaker had held the WBC welterweight title. He won two more fights in 1997 to take his record to 26–0.

Oscar hasn't forgotten about his education, either. "I'd like to go back to school. I've encouraged kids to pursue an education because it's very important to me. I've developed my skills as a boxer. After that I've got to develop my mind." Oscar De La Hoya is truly a man with a lot to be proud of and even more yet to accomplish.

Oscar wants to be the first Hispanic boxer to win titles across six weight divisions.

Chronology

- Born February 2, 1973, to Joel and Cecilia De La Hoya
- At age six, fought in first boxing match
- October 28, 1990, mother died of breast cancer
- Attended the 1992 Barcelona Olympics for the U.S. Boxing Team and won a gold medal
- November 24, 1992, professional boxing debut
- March 5, 1994, won first title as a lightweight in the World Boxing Organization (WBO) by beating Jimmi Bredaho
- June 7, 1996, beat Julio Cesar Chavez for the World Boxing Council (WBC) super lightweight title
- April 12, 1997, beat Pernell Whitaker for the WBC welterweight title

Index